MW01688999

Agoraphobia

How I Overcame This Crippling Disease

Adele Paolino

Apollo Books
263 W. 5th Street
Winona, Minnesota 55987

Library of Congress Card Number: 83-090117
ISBN 0-9611448-0-7

Publisher/Editor:
Adele Paolino
P.O. Box 92
Ft. Tilden, N.Y. 11695

Cover photo by Adele Paolino, Photojournalist

Manufactured by Apollo Books, 263 W. 5th St., Winona, MN 55987

PRINTED IN THE UNITED STATES OF AMERICA

$5.95

Dedication

To those who know the pain...

"It's the Soul Afraid of Dying That Never learns to live..."

From "The Rose" Sung by Bette Midler

Contents

Introduction

"Agoraphobia." It is a disease that cripples the mind like Polio once crippled limbs. Although a person afflicted with Agoraphobia has limbs that function normally, their mind plays miserable tricks on these limbs, freezing them immobile at the thought of leaving their front door. But today, like Polio, there is a cure for Agoraphobia.

In this book, through personal reflections and technical data, I have learned throughout my nine year bout with this disease, I describe my personal reflections and experiences with agoraphobia, how I began to recognize my symptoms and my search for help in dealing with my anxiety attacks.

Told in simple, easy-reading style, integrated with quotes from other agoraphobics I have met through my research, support group, mail and in phone conversation, I discuss how I completely recovered, how today I run an International Pen Pal Club for Agoraphobics with hundreds of members, a busy Hotline service, co-moderate an Agoraphobic Support Group with Dr. Stephan Fox, PH.D., C.S.W., and take agoraphobics out into the feared situations as a phobic aid, as well as hold down a part-time job as Contributing Editor of a Queens, N.Y. newspaper, *The Wave,* and, Editor of an International Newsletter, *Personally Yours News* for agoraphobics.

Through my research I have found that there is a common denominator in all agoraphobics. We are all highly loving, over emotional, super-sensitive, very intelligent people, who are constantly striving for perfection in ourselves to the point of excessive browbeating, self-inflicted low esteem and self- destruction.

In the book's conclusion, I stress how I recovered from my torment with no regret of ever having it. Agoraphobia must be felt in it's entirety before one can understand it or help others suffering from it.

In spite of the nightmare I once lived in the grip of

Agoraphobia, this disease has brought me a richness of life and an abundance of friends I never knew existed, and I would not have missed the experience for the world!

Chapter One

First "Anxiety Attack"

I gazed up at the kitchen clock; 11:30, almost lunchtime. I had to get to the supermarket. The refrigerator was once again bare. The baby needed milk, and what was I going to make for dinner, never mind lunch? My nerves were shot. Worry—Worry, why did I always have to worry so much? Why couldn't I find shopping enjoyable like Joanne and Maria? A simple task seemed to throw me into a frenzy!

The familiar pain was radiating through my lower extremities and my monthly flow was getting heavier by the minute. The cramps were so bad I felt I was going to double over. My legs felt heavy, and my head began to pound. This couldn't be all in my mind like my doctor said——I felt terrible! Yet, the grocery list was beckoning. There was no one else to do it since Benjie was only two, and my husband Ben, was working late.

"Be a responsible woman, Adele. For once take control!" I told myself. I popped a pill in my mouth. Dr. Hayes said it would help the cramps.

"It's called, Darvon Compound." He added, "Take it with milk, it may cause nausea."

I didn't like the way it made me feel. The pill not only made me nauseous, but it seemed to also have a strange effect on my nervous system too. Great——just what I needed, a pill that made me more nervous! But, I took it anyway. It had to be safe, after all, my doctor wouldn't give me anything that would harm me, would he?

I convinced myself it would work by the time I got to the store and then I'd lie down for awhile when I got home.

I put Benjie in his stroller, and off I went.

It was a 95 degree, thick August day. The mugginess made me feel like I couldn't breathe. The two blocks of walking to the store seemed to never end. I was becoming increasingly flushed, perspiring profusely, and more and more nauseous. I felt like I was going to vomit, and the cramps weren't getting any better either.

Once at the store, I ran through the aisles of the supermarket, dizzy, disorientated with palpitations coming on, I threw the needed items in my basket. Benjie was riding along with me in the seat up front of the cart, giggling. I was finding it hard to concentrate on his little laughing face, which was starting to blur. The products on the shelves were closing in on me.

I tried to concentrate, and bumped into my friend, Valerie. She began talking to me about something, I don't know what————I only knew I had to get out of the store fast! Making a feeble excuse to my friend, I hurried to the checkout counter. My legs were like jelly, my ears began to ring strangely, and the line never seemed to budge ahead.

I blacked out.

When I finally came to, I was in an ambulance and there was an oxygen mask on my face. I panicked.

"Where's my baby? What happened?"

The ambulance attendant reassured me that I merely fainted, but my blood pressure was low and they were taking me to the hospital just to get me checked over.

"But, my baby . . . ."

"Don't worry," he assured me. "Your girlfriend, Valerie knew how to contact Ben at work and she took Benjie home with her. Your husband is meeting us at the emergency room."

Ben looked worried as they wheeled me into the busy hospital room. I couldn't breathe, and was sure I was having a heart attack.

The doctor checked me over thoroughly and assumed I was much too young at the age of twenty-six to be having a heart attack and that I was fine. He then gave me an injection of valium for my nerves and said we could go home. He told my husband I was suffering from "anxiety", and gave me a prescription for mild tranquilizers.

I felt so embarrassed and ashamed for having lost control, collapsing like that——.

An incredible crippling fear overtook my mind, and I never went back to the supermarket again for almost two years! I was petrified that if I did, the horrible nightmare would all happen again. I thought I was going crazy. I didn't know what was wrong with me. What kind of woman as I anyway? The guilt of not being able to do a simple thing like shop for my family's needs was staggering.

The fear became an obsession. I was bitter, resentful, hated myself for being weak, but I couldn't help it. I just froze with fear at the thought of leaving my home ever again. Day after day, I became more and more depressed.

God! What is happening to me? I prayed for a cure, but there was no help available for me. I was doomed to an asylum where I belonged with all the other crazy people. I was surely going mad!

I didn't know at the time that I was merely suffering from a disease called, "Agoraphobia" and there was a simple cure!

Chapter Two

What Is it? How Do You Get It?

"Agoraphobia" is a Greek word which means fear of the marketplace, and/or open spaces. It can mean literally a fear of public places. It is an incapacitating anxiety on traveling away from the safety of home, or on being in crowded places such as churches, theatres, restaurants, schools, bridges, tunnels, escalators, elevators, trains, buses, planes, or of being in any situation where the sufferer thinks she may experience overwhelming panic, weakness, dizziness, giddiness, nausea, palpitations, or an "anxiety attack" where she will make a fool of herself in front of others or to be unable to get help quickly. She has an overwhelmed feeling upon these physical symptoms and has the uncontrollable urge to turn back to the place, usually home, where she feels safe again.

She avoids going back to that place, or any place like it, in fear that if she does, she will once again be overcome by these feelings. If the first attack came while she was driving on a parkway, she will avoid driving on parkways, then avoiding all roads, leading to avoiding all travel. Usually the farther she is away from home, the worse she feels and her environment or horizons become smaller and smaller. She feels anxious anywhere except in her house, sometimes in her own room. She becomes totally housebound. Her greatest fear is of the panicky feelings themselves, and avoiding them becomes her principle preoccupation, so much so, she makes up constant excuses, and desperately tries to hide, and cover her fears from everyone, sometimes even herself. She begins to think she is going mad.

Her principal fears are fear of collapsing, fainting, screaming, standing in line, being paralyzed in the street, being alone in the house, talking with someone and being "trapped" by their conversation, childbirth, physical illness, a heart attack, even death.

This results in becoming sensitized to these feelings and one flash of panic quickly follows another. Each flash then mounts in intensity from excess adrenalin she's producing in her own system with fear. This panic is the main reason why a phobic becomes reluctant to go into any situation where she fears a re- current attack will follow the first. Her imagination runs overtime with these dreaded situations. The "what if" syndrome begins and she only has to think fear to bring fear on. This of course then leads to the physical symptoms which she is afraid of in the first place, and every anxious thought brings on a flash of a panic leading to more anxiety and the obsession of this fear brings on a cycle of sensitization-fear-sensitization, and now there is a pattern and development of permanent agoraphobia. To be cured, she must then learn how to de-sensitize herself from these fears and learn how to master certain techniques, (which I discuss in a later chapter) and practice these techniques over and over again.

It is sometimes called "the housewives' disease" because many women who have been constantly home and later venture out again find the world to be gobbling them up and can't cope after being sheltered in the safety of their homes for a long period of time. However in the last five years of my research of agoraphobics, I have found many very young, single women who lose jobs, boyfriends, and all hopes for ever marrying in the future, and have met men who suffer from this disease too. The men find it most debilitating when they fear traveling away from home; jobs, dating and their masculinity are tremendously threatened in these cases.

Out of the current population in the United States of 226.5 million, 26 million are estimated agoraphobic by figures from the phobia clinics. But how many more are hiding behind closed doors, afraid that they are going insane?

Recent findings state that 80% of all whom seek help are cured today. We have also found through research that this ailment seems to come to full surface in times of stress, loss, illness or confinement for long periods of time.

We sometimes don't know what it is that triggers agoraphobia, but in my case, as well as in many other's whom I've researched, I was probably born agoraphobic, or I acquired it through osmosis from my parents.

Many, of whom I interviewed, also seemed to remember unpleasant memories in their childhoods that could have caused their insecure feelings that later took the form of this disease.

When I look back on my childhood memories, all of the listed here seemed to be contributing factors to my acquiring this miserable disease.

I never traveled very far from home as a child. My parents owned a small grocery store and worked seven days a week there, never vacationing because they were simply "too used to working." We lived upstairs from the store. So it was down to the store mornings, and after the days' work was over, it was back upstairs evenings. My mothers' parents conveniently lived in the same building. My fathers' parents lived only a few blocks away. There was no need to travel very far to visit with grandparents.

I never knew what it was like to have to go shopping with my mother in a supermarket or department store like other little girls did, because she simply didn't have to. My uncle owned a fruit and vegetable store on the same block, and there were a line of little specialty shops all in a row, whose owners all became family friends in this very traditional "Italian neighborhood of the '50's". There was a hardward store, baker, butcher, small family clothing store, even a toy shop on my block. The doctor was around the corner, the dentist a block down the road. The bank was across the street and my school was also around the corner. It was all so convenient to become a sheltered child!

My father never owned a car. He didn't have a need to. There was nowhere he had to go except the store. Other relatives merely visited with us. I remember also hearing my mothers' fears as a child. She fell once on the ice going to the bank, so on cold days thereafter she was afraid to go to the bank. On hot days she was afraid to wait in lines because she was afraid she'd faint from the heat. She was afraid to sit in church, a restaurant, movie, hairdresser, etc. My mother being merely a worrier, the doctors labled her a neurotic and had her hospitalized for valium withdrawal after addicting her on them in the first place. They almost put her through shock treatment which I stopped later on in my adult life when I realized she too was agoraphobic, not "physicotic or schizophrenic" as they tagged her.

In those days a woman didn't work. She was raised with the facts that a woman's place was at her husband's side, or in the home with the children. My mother never had to leave the confines of her home to be at my father's side or with her children as well as their business. There just wasn't any need to. So, when she found herself in any other strange environment other than the one she was used to, she panicked and sometimes got an anxiety attack. Unfortunately in those days, many women were carted off to the mental wards because doctors didn't know how to treat them. There wasn't any knowledge of agoraphobia and its' simple treatment.

If you look in "old readers" from which children learned from in the 1940's up until the 1960's, you'll see stories where the little girl was always pictured behind curtained windows waving goodbye to her hero, the little boy who was off to save her from some dangerous plight.

We were taught from little children that the girls' place was at home, and the boys' place was to go out to war, work, and to be his woman's savior. We became dependent on man for our every whim. It's no wonder that women of today find it so hard to "undo" these ties. Today's women who were brought up in the 40's to 60's with old ideals, find it the hardest to find freedom without guilt.

The age category for agoraphobics is anywhere from the early 20's to late 60's and 70's. The women in the 20 to 40 year old group seem to be able to recover quicker. These women are usually found in the 80% group of recovered phobics. It's the women in the late 50's and 60's age group that seem to find recovery the hardest, having been agoraphobic for so long with no help, and who have carried a burden of guilt with them from past years of old standards and ideals.

The small percentage of men suffering from this disease, seem to always recover with proper training on coping with feared traveling insecurities because theirs' never seem as deeply rooted as women's guilts, although the guilt is there. Men seem to be able to bounce out of agoraphobia more quickly though, and they somehow cope better with their physical symptoms, although there are exceptions.

My mother was lucky, she is fine today. And I was lucky too. I found treatment before I landed in an institution, on drugs, or alcoholic through the support of many other agoraphobics I met through phobic clinics, groups and through the mail. I found the secret of recovery was in sharing, caring, support and practice with other agoraphobics who understood what it felt like to suffer from this disease.

Chapter Three

An Agoraphobic's Childhood and Development

When I think back now, I thought I was alone with my fears. I thought I was the only one in the world with such strange feelings of uneasiness when away from the shelter of my comfortable home. It would be years before I found out I wasn't crazy, odd or alone. It was only a year ago that I learned I wasn't an oddity and millions of women shared my fears and were also hiding them because they were afraid to tell anyone their deep, dark, horrible secret.

Many stemmed from being in a parochial school.

Like myself, I later found that many women shared my background and that three out of every five agoraphobics were brought up in this strict environment.

When I started school, I remember my mother walking me there every day, right up to the fifth grade, even though the school was around the corner. She didn't mean to be over-protective, it was because she loved me that she refused to break the umbilical cord.

I remember too, the first day, the horrible feeling in the pit of my stomach, when she waved good-bye and I had to finally fend for myself in a new strange world that I later learned to hate. I never felt comfortable in school. I always wanted to go back home.

It was thought best for me to go to this school, not only because it was nearby, but because it was a good school and the nuns were supposed to be better teachers, even though I wanted to be with my little friends from my block, who went to public school.

The one thing I got to learn from the nuns was "discipline"!

Although things are much more liberal today in these schools, back in the early 1950's they taught you, I should say, brainwashed and drummed into you, that you had to be in total control of your mind, body and soul at all times and that it was a sin to lose control of yourself or your body functions because God made us into His image and likeness, which was perfection since God was perfect, which was a hard thing to be as a child.

One day when I was in the second grade, I raised my hand to leave the room at an undesignated time. Recess was at noon. It was only 10:30 and not the time for me to lose any self-control. I was upset and kept raising my hand that it was an emergency. I was locked in the clothes closet for being a pest. I wet my pants in the dark closet, and was sent home crying. I was no longer perfect. I had lost control of myself and was severely punished by the nun for not holding myself as a disciplined child of God. For the rest of the term, the nun tormented me and treated me as the devil himself. I was never the same after that. I began to feel insecure of myself more and more.

I hated sitting through the long hour masses that were a requirement to attend as a child. The church was dark, like the closet, and I was constantly afraid of having to go to the bathroom there. It had become a learned response to my first bad experience. I thought about the fear and my nerves produces a "real situation" of the physical symptoms and I actually panicked myself into this feared situation every time. I thought I was going to have to go to the bathroom in church, so I had to. This lasted throughout my life thereafter and I finally stopped going to church in my adulthood. Finally I then learned how to deal with this irrational fear and later could help others in my group suffering with it.

In my research, I learned Mary, a 50 year old housewife and mother of a grown daughter, shared my feelings and thought the nuns were cruel teachers that taught a hard class. "My parents being separated, I was raised in a Catholic home. I remember being put down in a dark cellar when I didn't know my work. My childhood memories are very unhappy and I grew up to be so shy and fearful."

Today she is fighting her daily fears of being alone since her daughter married and left home. When her husband is at work, she gets physical symptoms of palpitations, and weak spells. But by reaching out to others and understanding why she has these symptoms, she has started on the road to recovery. Being in a group, Mary has learned it takes time and practice to overcome these fears of the loneliness and "closed in" feeling associated with being locked in a cellar as a child.

The nuns were notorious for posing guilt on children. They slapped your head against the blackboard if you didn't know the answer to a question, and were demeaning and unsupportive. If you did good, they never praised you, only worked you harder. And if you did bad, that's when you were put down. They treated you like an imbecile, so you felt like one.

Pat, a mother of two, and 40 year old housewife, suffered terrible guilt for not being able to attend church. "I had terrible guilt and would try, really try to attend church when I became agoraphobic. I'd start on Friday dreading the approaching Sunday. Often I'd get there, but at the very last minute I'd back out. I guess it was my basic fundamental upbringing. They preached a lot of 'hellfire and brimstone' and that so many things were wrong, the slightest infraction of God's rules would doom you forever. I was very timid and withdrawn as a child. It took me years and years to learn that God is a God of Love." Pat suffered her first anxiety attacks as an adult while singing in a church choir and had to quit the one thing she truly enjoyed because of these attacks. As the symptoms progressed, she no longer could go to church services or even drive to the church with her family. The guilt was devastating and went against the grain of all Pat's Christian teaching. Agoraphobia then took over her life and she could no longer go to theaters, restaurants, shopping, visiting or driving alone. Today Pat is one of my dearest and best friends. We met through a phobic newsletter. Step by step Pat charted her accomplishments on a calendar as she progressively got better, in red. She learned to appreciate her every little accomplishments and not browbeat herself when she was on a "down." Today Pat goes to church again, and is very active in a "self help" group for Agoraphobics in her state called, HOPE. She is very active and supportive in the pen-pal group of which she helped form today.

"I feel God has hand chosen me to have had suffered and recovered from agoraphobia to be His helping hand here on earth to teach others how to overcome this dread disease". She says.

There are a few of us too, having been brought up with nuns and have agoraphobia, who can shed some humor on the subject as Erleen, who has a PH.D. in microbiology put it. "Have you heard that there are three kinds of guilt? Real guilt, probable guilt and Catholic guilt?——It's supposed to be a joke, but I recently read that most of the phobic people are raised by nuns". She continues, "It sure makes you think . . ."

And Valerie, a housewife, mother of three and phobic for many years, said, "I've always thought that I could write a good story, 'Do Black Patent Leather Shoes Really Reflect Up?' This of course is the old joke about nuns forbidding girls to wear black patent leather shoes because they were too much like a mirror and boys could look up your dress!"

All of us, one way or another suffered from our childhood upbringing. But we later learned as adults either through therapy, support groups and behavorial modification that these feelings of guilt can be overcome.

Later in my adult life when I was learning how to recover from agoraphobia, I was asked to photograph a "High Mass" for a Pastor Friend of mine having graduated from the New York Institute of Photography. I hadn't been to church in years but I wanted the job and the challenge of it enough to say, "yes," I'd do it. A week before the scheduled Mass, I began to have terrible symptoms and nightmares of being a little girl again in a big, dark, church and having to go to the bathroom. The "what if's" began again.

"What if I'm taking the photos and I have to leave to go to the bathroom?" was all I could think about for that whole week. I applied every technique I had learned in the past years of dealing with my irrational fears, but somehow they just weren't working. However, I had learned that you must face the feared situation in order to conquer the fear, so I was determined I could make it!

It was a cold, snowy day, and I had a bulky coat on and my camera equipment when I walked into a very warm-brightly lit church. Not a thing like the one in my nightmares.

Father George came to me and took my hand, "Come with me, Adele, let me show you where to hang your things . . ." To my disbelief, he went on and on, he took me into the Sacristy and showed me around.

"Here is the closet for your things, and here is a sink, cups and some running water if you get thirsty——and oh, here (he opened a door) is a bathroom just in case you have to take a break——Lord help us, it will be a long mass . . . ."

Everything in reality was so different from my childhood memories. I felt so silly for having carried such an irrational fear around with me for so long.

I got through that mass fine, snapping away and doing a great job at that. I was able to go back to church again after that, and my faith has come back since.

When I shared this experience in our group with a male phobic, who is Catholic, and shared the guilt feelings of not being able to go to church because he was afraid that if he had to leave, all eyes would be on him in judgment, we were able to come to the conclusion that many of the people that stand at the back of the church near the door are suffering from the same agoraphobic problem. That's why they are near the door——just in case they have to make a speedy exit with no one to see they left. But how irrational this fear is. No one, including God will mind if you MUST leave and there basically are no rules or commandments of God that state, "Thou shall not leave Church if you feel sick." When you change the, "What if I must leave," to "So what if I must leave," you'll see how irrational it all is. And the fact is, no one will really judge you or notice you if you do leave. The only one feeling guilt about your not getting through a whole mass is you! So be kind to yourself and let it ride. The next time you'll see how much easier it will be to stay the whole time if you want to.

How easy the rest of my life would have been if I had known this and how to cope with the irrational teachings of the nuns.

The browbeating I was taught as a little girl got only worse as a teen. I wanted to be with my friends in a public school, but my mother and grandmother wanted to keep me away from boys and have me pure as the driven snow until my wedding day, so they sent me to an all girls convent school.

Once again, the disciplinary measures taken there led me to become more withdrawn from the personality I could have been developing-a normal one-if I had been free from these women in black.

Here we were not even allowed to talk from the time we got in school, until we left. Lunch period was a bore sitting next to other girls and not being able to talk about any of the latest "in things" teens need so much to share.

We were taught it was a sin to kiss a boy, go near a boy or

even look at one. We would burn eternally in hell. We were taught to always be in control. If we were sick, there were sly looks and remarks. We were looked upon as a weak woman. If we complained of pain with our period, we were ridiculed. Gym period had to be taken with or without pain. To give into "imaginary pain" was to be scorned.

There were a few times I found myself sprawled across the lunchroom floor having fainted. At one time I had mononucleosis and was totally unaware that it had been advancing fast and affecting my liver because I was afraid to go to the doctor for treatment and miss school and get into trouble. I went to school with high fever and hid my illness very well until I was put into the hospital and was then out of school for six months.

When I returned everyone looked at me like I was wearing a scarlet "A" on my chest! I became frightened every time I didn't feel well and had to go to school thereafter. I began to retreat to my room and never wanted to leave it. I even began playing hookey and "hid" in my basement the fear and hatred of school became so intense.

I just couldn't face the embarrassment of getting sick away from the confines of my home. I sat in the bathroom for hours before leaving for school forcing myself to have a bowel movement, because I knew that if I had to go in school I wouldn't be allowed to.

Dating became a nightmare.

When I was 17 I finally met Bobby and fell madly in love. He lived in my neighborhood. I decided that the garbage the nuns were filling my head with was just that——garbage. I loved Bobby and he loved me and I wasn't going to hell.

When he kissed me, I got butterflies all over. It was my very first love and my first conquest at love since he asked me to go steady. It was also my very first sexual experience and I used to feel faint just at his touch. When he held me, I sometimes got dizzy. I didn't realize at the time what I was feeling was a normal body urge, something to enjoy, not to be afraid of! These feelings scared me so much I began to fear even going on outings with him too far from home. I was petrified he would kiss me and bring on these feelings and I would faint and make a fool of myself.

One time he asked me to go upstate on a picnic with two other couples. I got an attack of diarrhea just at the thought of being so far away from home with him. Naturally I couldn't go. It got worse.

Every time he wanted to go to the beach or a ride somewhere I got panicky and made an excuse. The only thing I felt comfortable with him doing was watching television at home where I felt safe. Bobby being an adventurous, outgoing, healthy male left me. I couldn't blame him. I was a bore. Too bad Bobby didn't know I was more frightened of losing control of myself more than I was frightened of him!

The next man in my life was Don. He was thirty-three years old. I was nineteen at the time. I knew Don all my life. He lived across the street from me. He was mature, wealthy, good looking and had a beautiful new convertible car. He bought me expensive jewelry and swept me off my feet. We became engaged. The problem was, he introduced me to liquor. I had felt phobic at times with him, but we usually went out for a drink or two and it relaxed me. I unfortunately became used to having drinks to keep me calm when we were out. Later on in life I would rely on liquor as a crutch to drown my fears to the point of almost becoming an alcoholic.

My research later showed many agoraphobics turn to liquor to help them through their plight. But the question still remained, what came first, the agoraphobia or the alcoholism since alcohol can produce side effects similar to agoraphobia too.

When using alcohol as a crutch to get through social functions, Joan and Lynn had similar backgrounds and feelings about it.

Joan was married to her first husband from fifteen to twenty years of age, which produced two children. "I ran into that due to escape, I suppose, from my fifteen years of living with an alcoholic father and emotionally immature mother. I re-married at twenty-one, had another child, and was off on my new life of just following my husband during his growth and job changes, re- locations, etc." She continued, "When we started with cocktail parties, I found if I drank I'd embarrass myself, and if I didn't, I couldn't communicate with my husband's co-workers and their wives. I was so lacking in the social graces . . . ."

Lynn added, "That's exactly how I felt about liquor. For awhile it was great, than I needed alcohol when I was in places it would be out of the question, like church and P.T.A. meetings. That's when I became acquainted with Librium and Valium."

Both Joan and Lynn, like myself found that alcohol wasn't really solving anything and we were using alcohol to calm us when away from home so we could stay awhile. Tranquilizers didn't help either because after one pill wore off, you'd reach for another. Using alcohol as a crutch or a support was as dangerous as tranquilizers since it too is a drug and all drugs have effects that can sometimes even cause paranoia. No agoraphobic needed to add being paranoid to her initial problem!

Audrey, a sixty year old widow doesn't even go down to her mailbox anymore. She has everything sent up to her, including her booze. She says she drinks as much as a quart of vodka a day. "I know it's the alcohol that is making me too sick to leave my apartment, but no one cares about me, so I drink to cover my fears of leaving the house."

Audrey has to take the first step to want help before anyone can help her, but unfortunately she is probably one of the agoraphobics in the 20% category that can never be cured. Her alcoholism must be cured first, before we can even begin to help her agoraphobia.

Don and I broke up due to our age difference. Too bad however he left me with a bad habit, and I now depended on alcohol to keep me calm when I was out on a date.

And then I met Ben, my present husband of 12 years.

Chapter Four

Marriage, Motherhood And Permanent Fixture At Home

I fell in love with Ben from the very beginning and relied on having a few drinks when we went out to keep me calm and happy. But maybe it's because I really loved him and wanted to be with him every minute, no matter where, my phobias seemed to almost vanish at the time. I felt very comfortable with him and placed my life and all my well being into his hands. I trusted him so much. I would go to the ends of the earth with him, and for the first time in my life I did some traveling——phobia free.

We went to Puerto Rico, St. Thomas, Nassau, Catskills, and to Cape Cod. It was in Cape Cod we made the decision to live somewhere in a little cottage on the beach. After marrying, we found Breezy Point, a small beach town on the Jamaica Bay.

It was hard leaving my mother and father behind, but we were only an hour away and visited them frequently.

I loved my little house on the bay and it was very peaceful and serene here. But it was also very secluded. I depended on Ben to take me shopping, to the dentist, and later the doctor when I found I was pregnant. I also had to learn how to shop in a supermarket and department store. It was all very new and strange, but even though I felt a little uneasy shopping, I sometimes really enjoyed it.

Benjie came the hard way. Although my pregnancy was a normal one, I ended up having him by Caesarean Section after 18 hours of hard labor. It was a very frightening experience. One I never wanted to repeat since the two of us almost died in childbirth. A fear of future pregnancies cropped up at this point. So another fear was added to my growing list. Also guilt was overtaking me every time someone asked, "Aren't you going to give Benjie a playmate?" And, "You're not going to let Benjie be an only child are you?"

I later met Bella, and she too shared my fear and guilt. She was given so many drugs during her child's birth she became agoraphobic and severely housebound. She was afraid of drugs and didn't take so much as aspirin in fear of getting an agoraphobic attack. She felt guilty not giving her husband the son he so much wanted, but she just couldn't go through all the agony of it all again.

So, I settled in my little cottage, baby, daddy, and mommy made three. Only mommy was becoming too comfortable at home and hardly ventured out much except to walk the baby on the beach on nice days, and my big outings to the supermarket for survival!

Now I no longer even went there.

After fainting in the store that day, I became completely housebound, and more and more depressed.

I did try a few times to walk the long blocks to the supermarket, but my legs never seemed to get me there. I always turned back and asked Ben to pick up things on his way home from work. On his day off, he would do the heavy shopping for me. I always had an excuse. I was too tired, had my period . . . .

I hated myself and became very nervous. I began to drink to calm myself, never a lot, but enough. It seemed the day after I had a couple of vodka and tonics, I felt more disorientated and was afraid to leave my home and fall on my face.

Ben became so worried about my condition, he took me to a doctor who ran some blood tests on me. He said I had hypoglycemia, or low blood sugar and put me on a special diet.

I didn't realize at the time that there is approximately five teaspoonsful of sugar to every ounce of alcohol, plus a lot of sugar in the tonic water. So, I was playing havoc with my blood system with my drinking as well. Sugar, in too high a quantity was a no-no for my system. Most of these symptoms were physical which led to my mental fears. Ironically many agoraphobics that I later researched were suffering a combination and sometimes all three, and were agoraphobic, alcoholic and hypoglycemic!

Hypoglycemia can cause many of the same symptoms as an agoraphobic attack and the two can be related. Many agoraphobics are unaware that they may have low blood sugar. Hypoglycemia is opposite diabetes. The pancreas becomes overactive and produces too much insulin. A diabetic needs insulin to help the pancreas produce more sugar which the body needs. So, the effects of hypoglycemia are the same as a diabetic having an overdose of insulin, i.e., shock, dizziness, nervousness, cold sweats, shakiness, anxiety and even collapse.

In his book, *Low Blood Sugar And You* Dr. Carlton Fredricks states, " . . .for one person in every ten, sugar is a deadly food, paving the way toward a hundred distressing physical symptoms, plus all the tortures of neurotic and even psychotic behavior."

Alcohol is pure distilled sugar.

Also, more than eight in every ten hypoglycemics have a ravenous appetite for sweets, since an overactive pancreas spurs the desire for sweets and is re-instilled and stimulated again when sugar is eaten. So, the more sugar you put into your body, the more you crave. For example: Overweight people who are in the cookie, cake and ice cream binge—— the more they eat, the more they crave, etc.

Dr. Fredricks continues, " . . .such a strong desire for sugar is also characteristic in alcoholics who alternate between periods of sobriety and intoxication. The quantities of candy they can consume while sober are unbelievable and offer a clue to low blood sugar . . . ."

So too, the more you drink, the more you crave another drink . . . overworking your pancreas, causing your body to feel like you're on a constant roller coaster ride.

Stress, which is common in agoraphobics, can also be a contributing factor in hypoglycemia; the more stress we are under, the more our blood sugar, like blood pressure can rise. Alcoholics are also under constant stress, physical and emotional.

Most hypoglycemics are put on a high-protein, low carbohydrate diet and vitamins. This diet consists of eating only meat, fish, eggs, cheese, vegetables, fruits, wheat bread, milk, light tea, caffeine-free coffee, and sugar free soft drinks. The trick is to stay away from sugar and starches such as while bread, cake, cookies, macaroni, pizza, sweet colas and mostly caffeine. B Vitamins and Dolmite, which is a natural tranquilizer and natural fructose, (a sugar substitute) works wonders!

After I had been on this diet awhile, and free from alcohol, I was amazed how much progress I made in my recovery. I shared this in common with two women I met through the White Plains Phobia Clinic, Arlene, a 33 year old housewife and mother of two, who had been agoraphobic for nearly four years, who had tried drinking to bring down her anxiety, found that it not only made her depressed but that everything she ate or drank with sugar in it made her anxiety worse. "I finally went to a doctor and he eliminated all sugar in my diet." Arlene is now able to travel again and recently took a very exciting trip. "I find I can cope with almost anything now and I'm recovering quickly from my agoraphobia since I'm on a sugar free diet. . . . " she said proudly!

Diane, agreed with both Arlene and me. "When I was in college, I drank a lot of tequila and dieted off and on. Then I came down with mononucleosis and had my first anxiety attack which came out in full bloom. My doctor took a Glucose Tolerance test on me and found I had one of the severest forms of hypoglycemia that was affecting me psychologically. He put me on a diet and vitamins, and I think I have cracked a hole in the mystery of agoraphobia...even allergies can play havoc on the agoraphobic system.

Since most agoraphobic women are between the ages of 20 to 70, it takes in another category of stress, which is menstruation, pre-menstrual tension and menopause!

Pre-menstrual tension is one of the worst problems of a phobic and can create havoc on "those" days, like what happened to me in the supermarket on my first anxiety attack.

Dizziness, faintness, cold sweats, nausea, headaches, hot flashes, blurring vision, lack of coordination, lethargy, mood swings, depression, anxiety, restlessness, irritability, tension, these are all symptoms of pre-menstrual tension and also menopause. On these days we should not push ourselves into the outer limits. We should be easy on ourselves, pamper ourselves and not brow-beat ourselves if we can't accomplish what we want to.

In my case, the day I fainted, it was a mixture of the pain and the reaction to the outside temperature as well as the side effects of the Darvon Compound, which was wrong for my system. I know that now, I didn't know it then. Today great strides are being made in helping women cope with menopause as well as pain in menstruation. It is not all in your head. The pain is real. Many women, 60% in all, suffer from too much of the hormone, progesterone, This causes the cramps. Today there are drugs like, Motrin, Ponstel, and Zomex, which work on the prostiglytin hormones that cause the cramps without any side effects. A woman need not suffer today, but she should take her pre-menstrual mood swings and physical discomforts into stride and take it nice and slow those days. Instead of shopping, if you can, take a bath and read a novel with your feet up!

As for myself at the time, I was confused with all my body non-functions and on a vicious merry-go-round of drinking, waking up with those hypoglycemic symptoms, pre-menstrual and menstrual symptoms, so, I stayed in the house and became agoraphobic, lost all my self-esteem and drank again. My blood sugar was going up and down like a yo-yo. I felt terrible. I stayed in seclusion and kept repeating this terrible cycle until I got smart.

It took some time however before this happened. The more I felt scared of becoming sick outside my home, the more I locked myself in it. I had made a prison for myself, and stayed in the only place I felt safe. I finally had to resort to a babysitter to take Benjie for walks, home delivery food service and catalog shopping.

And then one day I had to leave the confines of my home. My grandmother died.

Getting to the funeral mass was a disaster. I shook for the whole hour ride by car. When I finally got to the church, the inevitable happened. My childhood fears enveloped me. I got a diarrhea attack, threw up and passed out all at the same time it seemed.

I had my husband take me home, shaking all the way. But now a new symptom was developing. I couldn't catch my breath and felt like I was constantly suffocating.

I locked myself up in my room day after day, rocked myself to sleep. But sleep was even getting harder to find. I was an emotional wreck. Ben called a psychologist friend to the house.

His theory was that when I saw my grandmother closed in her coffin, I got the reaction of not being able to breathe. I was under stress, it would pass. He said it was a normal reaction.

But it wasn't normal, I got worse. I stayed in bed all day. I didn't care to get up, dressed, or even cook for my family. I just looked at the brick wall in my bedroom for hours. I finally came to the conclusion that the inevitable was about to happen and like my mother I too would end up in a hospital with a complete nervous breakdown, or worse I would end up in an institution for the mentally insane and locked up there.

This obsession, depression and depletion of self worth was leading to the next final step,——thoughts of suicide.

Although Ben tried to understand, he just couldn't. He kept pushing me to go out and kept yelling at me—— "Knock it off! Just go! Fight it!" But he couldn't know how the panic paralyzed me. I couldn't even visit my parents anymore. There was a Christmas and Easter when I stayed home all alone while Ben took the baby to visit and get his gifts. I told my parents I had the flu. I was full of excuses by now, and used every one in the book.

Finally Ben laid it on the line, "I may as well be divorced! I feel like I take my son out visiting once a week on my visitation rights. I have a wife, and want to go out as a family unit. Damn you, snap out of it Adele, or I'm leaving you!"

He was making my guilt worse, but even this didn't scare me into leaving my home and venturing back out. I just couldn't! I begged him to stay and help me. But how could he help me if I didn't even know how to help myself at the time?

I later met many women who lost husbands to divorce because of their agoraphobia and many young women lost boyfriends who couldn't understand why they feared certain dates or outings away from home.

Today through research we've found it is best for both the husbands or boyfriends and women involved with the male agoraphobic to attend the group sessions or individual sessions with the phobic at assigned times from the therapist to insure total understanding of what the agoraphobic is feeling, and how they as a partner can help the phobic overcome these feelings of anxiety as well as how to help them through anxiety attacks by relaxation methods. Alcoholics Anonymous and Al-Anon have proven in their research how much the suffering person can benefit by their spouse, family or loved ones understanding and helping them cope. It is also beneficial to the latter if he or she really cares and wants to help his phobic loved one.

Although the threat of divorce hung over my head, I just couldn't leave the house no matter how hard I tried. I literally froze at my doorstep. I had by now, learned to do all my chores with the telephone and through the mail. I phoned for food, clothing and daily needs and became very good at it. I was even able to get books to read through the yellow pages and book clubs. If I saw a book I wanted to read, I'd call the local book store and have it mailed to the house. It was more expensive that way, but I wanted to read something——anything to keep my mind from vegetating, and was totally incapable at the time of going to a library, nor the corner bookstore for a magazine, so I subscribed to them all!

I got lucky. I saw a book in a catalog called, *Peace From Nervous Suffering* by Dr. Claire Weeks. It seemed to be the type of book that could help me, so I sent for it.

It wasn't until I finally read it, that I found what the name was for what I was suffering from. I had all the symptoms of a disease called, *agoraphobia*.

I told Ben all about it. There was hope for me after all, and I asked him for his support. He agreed.

Actually at the time I didn't know it then and do now, Ben had been treating me absolutely right when he tried to push me into going out, although his methods needed some polish and tact.

However, although he seemed cruel in these tactics, I needed someone who was generally supportive, caring and made me face my fears, expose them to me gently without letting me back away from them, and letting some time pass to let me become accustomed to the feared situation once more; his constant shouting, loss of patience and threat of divorce was what made me retreat in fear back to my room even more.

The key here to a good buddy or phobic aid is an equal amount of sterness and sympathy.

I studied Dr. Weeks' book and read it over and over again. I just had to recover. I tried to put the doctor's methods into practice. But I felt I just couldn't do it alone. It seemed easy enough on the pages so I tried to put the principles into effect over and over again.

But it isn't as easy as it seems to learn how to de- sensitize yourself to these feelings, expecially when you're out in the feared situation and panic strikes. Without proper practice of this method, the phobic becomes disorientated and blurs out everything she has learned. It takes time and practice to overcome the panic. It took me five years, in a long hard struggle and a lot of help from other agoraphobics along the way to understand these basic principles which follow Dr. Weeks' book.

Dr. Weeks' method to a cure was said to come only when you faced the fact that you were agoraphobic and accepted this fact. Learning to float past the feelings when they arrived and letting time pass.

At the beginning, I never thought this was possible and the concept would never work for me. I couldn't seem to get the "floating" down and found it especially frustrating to do this when I was frozen with fear and my mind couldn't concentrate on these steps.

But it did work. Later——much later, and then I too was able to teach these methods to other agoraphobics in my work.

But at the time I had realized what was wrong with me, and was trying to put the principles of Dr. Weeks' book into effect, I had already been totally housebound for almost three years. Old habits are hard to break, but Benjie was now five years old and I had to face the fact that he had to go to school, and I had to take him there. I didn't drive, but there was a schoolbus that stopped for the children a block away. The first day of school, waiting for the bus to come was a nightmare for me. Something that should have been a pleasant day to remember——my son's first day of kindergarten, sent me trembling in anticipation, while my son was jubilant about the excitement of leaving home, traveling on a bus and going to school. My legs shook as I walked up the block with him. I was glad at least my little boy was together, because I certainly wasn't!

Once at the bus stop the waiting was endless. A few girls stopped to talk, I made idle chatter but I felt that if the bus didn't come soon they were going to scrape my remains off the ground!

Any friends I did have in the past, no longer called for me to go on outings anymore, and I later found out that everyone thought I was a snob because I didn't mingle. They never would have guessed I was scared to ruin their fun or let them see me get an attack and I felt they would never understand even if I tried to explain my problem. So I remained a hermit.

At the bus stop that first morning, I could see the odd looks on the other women and their surprise that I had showed my face around. One of them asked me where I kept myself, and that she never saw me in the supermarket or the park anymore. I made a feeble excuse like always——"I kept very busy at home, we probably just miss each other in transit . . . . "

There were days when it was impossible to walk Benjie to the corner and I had to get an older child from the next block to call for him on the way. Parent Teacher's meetings were impossible too. I couldn't go. The memories of school were all too miserable for me to conjure up again and I would never have been able to sit in a crowded auditorium. I sent Ben on all these chores. I, of course, stayed home feeling guilty. What kind of mother was I anyway?

I remember a day when the teacher called me to have me pick Benjie up because he was running a temperature. I didn't drive at the time, couldn't take a bus with my phobia, so I sent a taxi to the school to pick him up. What that teacher must have thought of me!

Although I had read Dr. Weeks' book at least 100 times by now, I still couldn't get past my floating. I tried to expose myself to my fears, but I knew I needed trained help to get me over the rough-starting points. I called a couple of psychologists but couldn't afford their price per hour, and I had no one to take me to their office. Most were in the city, and with my fear I couldn't get past the front door, never mind travel to a psychologist's office!

I remembered this plight I was in when I met Dr. Stephan Fox, PH.D. C.S.W. about a year ago. When he asked me what one thing I thought he should do to help agoraphobics, I shouted at him almost——"MAKE HOUSE CALLS!" This was the basis of the beginning of my job today as phobic aid and his booming practice here in N.Y.C. and Queens and Brooklyn area.

But at the time that I was sick back in 1977, there were few clinics or doctors nearby even trained to help agoraphobics.

Luckily, however through a newspaper article I stumbled upon, my recovery really began in a very strange, but helpful way.

The article listed the White Plains Phobia Clinic, which is headed by Dr. Zane, and supervised by Doreen Powell. It was much too far for me to travel to with my confinement, but they were nice enough to send me material on Contexual Therapy and a monthly newsletter they run for agoraphobics, called the *P.M. News.*

It was through this newsletter I later helped other women, and also formed the international agoraphobic pen-pal list and hotline service I run today. It was also here I had my first encounter with another agoraphobic from another state who turned out to be my best friend today, Pat.

Pat had written all about her fears of church, restaurants, driving, and how her world had shrunk to the point that she had become totally housebound. She also shared my pain in trying to explain her fears to her husband.

She wrote:" . . .there were times in the supermarket when I'd have a panic attack and couldn't finish my shopping, but with my husband's support, encouragement and understanding I decided I'd come out of it somehow. I'd reached a point where I couldn't even walk around the block on some days, but I started walking just to the corner and back and then a little further. I tried to go back to church, but I never allowed myself to consider defeat if I couldn't make it. The next time I'd do better."

I grabbed a pen and paper and wrote Pat a letter. I didn't know where she lived because only first names were used in the newsletter, so I asked the editor, Judy, to forward my letter to Pat.

A week later I received my first letter from Pat. She was so supportive and kind. And this was the basis of recovery for me and later others, just knowing there were others out there suffering from the same problem who were caring, understanding and shared a special bond.

Pat shared with me how she learned to apply Dr. Zane's Contextual Therapy methods to her everyday exposure and practice in dealing with her feared situations. It seemed she had a good idea about keeping records of her accomplishments either on a calendar or in a diary or journal.

Step by step we learned how to put both Dr. Week's and Dr. Zane's methods into practice and support one another on our accomplishments.

Pat had been making steady progress and not only was back to church, but now practicing going into restaurants and was driving again....

"I started going into a local fast food restaurant, standing at the counter and ordering a sandwich and soft drink to take out. It was a monumental undertaking, but at last the food came, and I left to sit in my car." She then went inside the next time and stayed just long enough to have a sandwich and small drink sitting near the door for a quick escape. She continued, "Several times practicing this method, I thought I'd never make it, but I stayed with it. Finally I ate a full meal there alone and felt so proud. When I asked my husband to take me out to eat one night, he was ecstatic!"

Pat had learned what floating, and letting time pass meant and she could now practice in every other feared situation slowly with exposure methods until she had completely recovered and has today!

Chapter Five

Learning Recovery Techniques

Dr. Zane's Contextual Therapy consisted of six points being:

1. Expect, allow and accept that fear will arise.
2. When fear comes, stop, wait and let it be.
3. Focus on and do manageable things in the present.
4. Label your level of fear from 0-10. Watch it go up and down.
5. Function with fear. Appreciate your achievement.
6. Expect, allow and accept that fear will reappear.

Like Dr. Claire Week's cure, they were very similar. Dr. Week's "accepting the fear" was similar, and her "floating" was equivalant to Dr. Zane's second step.

Practicing these procedures was the hard part to accomplish in the beginning. It was the "un-learning" of bad memories and focusing on the "now" that was the trick.

As an agoraphobic we had to expect that fear would arise because we were programmed to "scare" ourselves in unfamiliar situations. This is where we had to "unlearn" self inflicted scare tactics.

An agoraphobic doesn't fear going to the store because she's afraid she may get hit by a car on the way, she fears literally scaring herself into a panic attack where she can't cope. So, she must expect this reaction and change the "what if's" to "so what". She must ask herself, "What is the worst thing that will happen to me? I'll get an attack, if I let myself get one!" Talking to herself is the first step into recovering because she is distracting herself from her thoughts of doom. This is when you learn steps three and four. By focusing on the present and counting from 0-10 on a scale of one being not so bad and attack, to 10 being a downright zinger, she can concentrate on other things other than her fears.

Some phobic aids teach using a rubber band on the wrist helps. When panic strikes, a snap on the rubber band can bring you back to the present.

Floating or waiting for the attack to pass is one of the hardest steps to conquer. Once it is accepted, she can function with the fear. This is what actually helps the agoraphobic recover when she can appreciate the fact that she has accomplished something.

I had been recovering for sometime, when I took my son shopping to Woolworth for his birthday party goodies. Parked outside the bank, I had an attack. I hadn't had one for quite sometime, but I had reached about a 6 on the scale. I sat, concentrated on the present, talked myself into the fact I was going to merely buy party goodies, the attack would pass soon. When it did subside, I went into the bank, withdrew my money and briskly walked to Woolworth. I didn't let myself think of being inside the store, until I was in it. Once there, the panic arose slightly again, but I continued focusing on my little boy's happy face while choosing his party things and kept in the present thought of his happiness. The panic subsided, we finished shopping and I returned home happy I didn't give into my panic.

Imagery is also a helpful step to recovery. As Pat did with the restaurant, Kate did with her fear of driving.

Kate, a forty year old woman had developed a fear of driving herself to work in her automobile, making her dependent upon family members and friends, creating an inconvenience. She practiced imagining:

1. Sitting behind the wheel of her car with an "understanding friend," who would keep her company.
2. Driving around the block in the company of her friend.
3. Driving a few miles back and forth with her friend.
4. Driving the route to work and back with her friend.
5. Sitting alone behind the wheel of her automobile.
6. Driving around the block alone.
7. Driving a few miles back and forth alone.
8. Driving the route to work and back alone on a non-working day.
9. Driving back and forth to work alone.

Her levels would go up and down while she imagined these steps. She practiced dealing with these levels at home and by the time it was time to do the actual practicing in the car with her phobic aid present, then alone, these levels of anxiety were nil. In fact she never even reached a 1 on the scale. She had desensitized herself by imagining the feared situation and working with herself in the comfort of her home first before challenging the real situation. She was so proud of her achievement, the fear soon vanished.

Systematic desensitization is another technique for replacing fear with relaxation in fear arousing situations. It combines relaxation with gradually increased exposure to frightening imagined stimuli. The person does not actually approach the feared object, or situation. In imagination and through the use of photographs she pictures herself gradually moving closer to the fear arousing situation. She learns to approach the imagined target situation with small steps leading toward the target for a few seconds of discomfort and does not move forward again until the imagined target feels once again comfortable to approach. She is relaxed and then exposes herself again to the feared stimulus. This continues until she learns to feel safe with the photograph, then relaxed with the situation she can "graduate" on to the real thing and practice again relaxing, approaching, and relaxing until she feels comfortable with the situation. For example:

Joan was petrified of crossing a bridge. She first drew a picture of the bridge and stared at it, imagining she were moving in her car toward it. She then drew her car on the bridge and stared and practiced through imagery, and she then drew the bridge again with her car leaving it. When she felt secure to tackle the real thing she went to the bridge, parked and just looked at it. Then she walked over the bridge and back (she got out of her car). Later she was ready to drive across the bridge with a friend, then meet a friend on the other side, and ultimately she was again able to drive across the bridge herself!

In a case where many things are feared, exposure to the least fear inducing stimulus is used to later climb the ladder to the highest or worst fear. One can make a list of things that are feared. The first being the worst and the last, the least feared situation. Start at the bottom of the list and check off each fear you've accomplished overcoming, and work your way up!

In my case, supermarkets were one of my worst fears, and church was exceptionally bad for me to handle. I started from the bottom, which was walking to the bus stop with Benjie. I later graduated to conquering the supermarket and to my surprise I even learned to drive, bought my own car and went back to school, then later volunteered my time as a phobic aid!

Now that Benjie was in school, I had a lot of time on my hands to practice, and I did. There were days I merely walked to the supermarket and stood outside it not even going in. Then I worked my way from buying one item to two, later to a full cart. There were times I did leave the cart full in the middle of the aisle and ran home, but the next day I'd do better.

I finally decided I had too much time on my hands and

needed a hobby. I always liked to write, so I decided to take a "home study" course in short story writing. To my surprise, I published my first story out, which was a love story. It proved I had a great imagination. I was determined now to use that imagination for better things than thinking of the "what if's" of my feared situations.

I published quite a few stories and was becoming confident with myself again. I was learning to shop in local stores, but was still relying on home food service as a protection just in case I couldn't shop. I did some shopping in small specialty shops where there were no lines to wait on and was still too frightened to have to stay in a store for long periods of time.

I remember reading a letter from a phobic on "supermarket strategy" which stated

". . . Many *PM News* readers probably view supermarkets as phobic situations. The February, 1982 issue of *Datamation*, a computer magazine, offers an explanation of why people shy away from supermarkets.

The article states that because we are so bombarded with stimuli, we cannot screen it out after awhile. The author writes that she did a survey on the A&P food chain and found people were walking into stores and walking out again without buying anything. She claims the reason for this was that shoppers were overwhelmed because 'there are too many things in the store to pick from, too many items to understand, too much knowledge to absorb', so they went down to the local grocery store to buy their basics.

It would seem that an overload of stimuli, if not the basic cause of the phobic's problem, does contribute to rising levels. Contextual Therapy's Step Five: Focus on and do manageable things in the present, could help confused patrons, phobic or not, filter out some of the excess stimuli. Getting interested in one or two items on the shelf could be a way of limiting the amount of input a shopper need contend with at one time."

The author's note read: "Readers, please comment. This

theory may also apply to those multi-leveled, sprawled out malls, where there is so much to look at that the experience is often overwhelming."

I wrote back and commented. My letter was published in the following month's *PM News*:

"In my opinion, as response to your Supermarket Strategy in the last issue, I feel that the concept of shoppers 'being overwhelmed because there are too many things to choose from causes confusion and tends to make the phobic run down to the local grocery store'... may not be the real problem. A phobic can be overwhelmed in a small grocery store as well.

I live two blocks from a small store where I experienced my first anxiety attack. I feel that it's the basic fear of scaring yourself no matter where you are that makes a phobic person go shopping in a store big or small and rush down the aisles flinging things into a basket and leaving as soon as possible.

Agoraphobics, in my opinion, would not stand still long enough to compare items for sale prices. They'll pay the price as long as they can get out quickly. I think they tend to go to their local grocery because it's just that——local—— and I don't think the amount of merchandise on the shelf really matters.

The same with malls. I wouldn't go to a mall or department store because first I'd have to travel there by car, bus, or train, and once there, would worry "what if" I get an attack——How would I get home fast?

I think the stimuli is confusing only within oneself... not the outside stimuli in choosing merchandise.

I must add, however, now that I've improved, I enjoy browsing through merchandise on my 'good days.' If I'm having a bad day, I don't risk going to a large store. I stay in a local, comfortable one."

This was true.

I had learned to get to the stores with jelly legs and all. I kept telling myself, "jelly legs will still get you there!" I'd pat myself on the back when I returned home with my packages and at the beginning I never pushed myself too hard for fear of a setback.

Agoraphobics when on the mend, fear having a setback, or another attack and landing back where they were at square one. For this reason we are taught to expect even setbacks and take them in stride. We are taught to rest, re-group and set right back out again into the feared situation only when we are ready to again.

I had my days of setbacks where I would set out and fail.. .but I kept practicing until I conquered. That's the only way to win agoraphobia over!

Chapter Six

Recovering

I was improving steadily, visiting my parents and Ben's family again plus shopping locally with my husband and son. I was ready to try a mall. Just the week before I had gotten a wonderful cash gift from my parents, and it was burning a hole in my pocket. "Buy yourself something, and while you're at it, here's something extra to buy Benjie some new clothes for school . . ." my mother said handing me an envelope.

I felt free from agoraphobia because I had learned from Contextual Therapy that I could cope with it now, so off I went bravely with my son to the shopping mall. I hadn't been there in over four years, although it is only ten minutes away from home.

When I walked in, I thought I was in dreamland. I was so excited going from store to store, people must have thought I had been locked away somewhere for years and had just been let out! In a way I had been——locked in my own prison that I made for myself, housebound and chained to my home.

I shopped, stood in lines, rode the escalators with no levels at all. My son was so happy, and he wondered what had happened to his mother, the one who made him look at pictures in catalogs, pick out his clothes and wait for the mailman to deliver them weeks later?

But then I began to feel faint and weak——but realized that my stomach was empty, looked at my watch and saw I had been in lines and shopping for nearly 2 1/2 hours and it was surely lunch time. I didn't panic, but realized I was merely tired and hungry and didn't give in to my physical symptoms. After lunch, I shopped for another two hours.

When I returned home from my shopping spree, I was exhausted and very happy. I looked at all the wonderful treasures I bought and smiled——and why not, I deserved them. It was my 35th Birthday and the first one I'd celebrate feeling free from agoraphobia.

I was beginning to learn the secret of overcoming this disease. With support and plenty of practice I knew now I was going to make it, and I did!

I began to feel that writing fiction was nice, but I wasn't getting out as much as I should either. I was busy and working, but I was working at home, alone, with my typewriter creating characters and making them come alive on blank pieces of paper. I was living the lives of my creations——not my own.

I was able to go to the library now too. So I read everything in sight. I decided to switch to article writing and within a few months covered a small story for my local newspaper.

Ben drove me to the newspaper office and to my surprise the Editor liked it and asked me if I'd write on a weekly basis for the paper and cover the happenings of the Breezy Point section, since there was no reporter in my area.

I nervously said I would although I had very little confidence in myself. I thought that the experience would be good for my recovery, and it did turn out to be a vital part of it too!

In a few months I was confident enough to accept the editor's request for a weekly column covering the social happenings on the beach. This led to my getting around my area and meeting people in my community on a regular basis. I was comfortable with my job because I was never too far from home and could always retreat back if I had to. Amazingly, I rarely did. Once I was out "covering" a story, I was totally involved in it and not in myself or my fears.

Then I decided I really wanted to learn to drive, get around more and be less dependent on Ben to take me to the newspaper every time I had a story to turn in. Ben agreed to teach me, and learning to drive, getting my license was one of the hardest parts of overcoming agoraphobia, but I didn't realize how strong I was becoming and how much I had improved in the last few years.

I was driving alone locally, when I got my first setback. I had been on my way to the newspaper to deliver my column, when I hit a ten on the scale. It had just come out of the blue, as I hadn't lost control this badly in years and was terrified when it struck.

My head was spinning, I couldn't breathe, and I felt I was going to faint. I pulled over and used all the tactics I had learned. I breathed, diverted my attention to my radio and tried to focus on what the man was talking about on it, then I saw an apple along side me. I reached for the apple using it as a diversion tactic and ate it. The attack subsided and I was able to get to the newspaper after that. My legs were still shaky, but I had made it. But from that time on, I never traveled without my new crutch, which was some sort of food, fruit or gum by my side.

Any "crutch" that makes you feel better in the beginning is great to use in combating agoraphobia. A crutch can be anything from a sympathetic friend, a crossword puzzle to distract oneself, or even medication. Like a real crutch, these devices do serve a purpose, and there comes a time when they can be discarded with progress in treatment.

Ann, a 30 year old phobic, got terrible attacks where her

mouth would get dry. She said she felt like she had cotton in her mouth, restricting her from breathing, and she got panicky when his happened driving her car away from where she could get a drink quickly. She stopped driving due to this fear, until she began taking a thermos of water along with her. Feeling again safe, with her "crutch", she later was confident to drive again.

Ernestine, a 36 year old housewife and mother of three, had always been a very active working woman, and was working in real estate for seven years before agoraphobia set in. "One summer day, eight years ago, agoraphobia surfaced, I wouldn't say it started, because I believe it had been present before that, I just never realized it. I thought I was losing my mind when it hit. I found I could no longer drive alone, not even one block and had to quit my job. It was the beginning of a living hell, and I was so ashamed to tell anyone . . . . "

Today Ernestine is doing much better since she's learned how to deal with agoraphobia. "My panic attacks come, but I'm able to deal with them. It hasn't been easy, but I'm gaining steps everyday. If the panic attacks come, I'm prepared for them and can cope." She says.

Learning how to cope was the key for us all in recovery. As for me, I had now decided I wanted to take pictures to go along with my newspaper articles, and since I was gaining ground, I decided to take a photography course.

I found school a lot different than when I went as a child, and I absolutely adored my teacher and looked forward to classes.

How proud I was when I graduated with diploma from the N. Y. Institute of Photography!

And now I could do newspaper assignments, and covered all kinds of interesting ones. I particularly liked one on a new medical building opening and did an interview with the dentist. In turn, I got my confidence back and went to him to get my teeth taken care of, which I had neglected for years because of my phobia.

I still got anxiety attacks as I well remember the day of my first dentist appointment. He had been running a little off schedule and I had been waiting for over 15 minutes, when my levels began to rise. By the time he was ready for me, I had hit a #10, and was ready to run out of the office. However, I had learned to stay with the attack and see it through and was very proud when my teeth were finished a few weeks later and I hadn't even cancelled one appointment!

Many of us are petrified of dentists and doctor's offices. Not because we are afraid of pain, our main fear as an agoraphobic is making a fool of ourselves in the office with an attack and wanting to run out.

Pat had had the problem with eye doctors and having to pick out a frame, but when she wrote, "I was able to pick out a very nice pair that were flattering with no level at all . . ." I was so darn proud of her and of me for having made the dentist!

Many women also had this problem with beauty parlors. I remember a day after I had set up my hotline number for phobics to call when in difficulty, when Carol called frantically.

" . . . I'm calling from the beauty parlor and I'm having an attack, what am I to do? The "goo" is on my head, and I have to sit with it on for another 20 minutes, and I'm shaking all over. I have to get out of here . . ." her voice was shaky.

I happened to know Carol quite well by now, and knew she had hypoglycemia. It was probably time for her to have a protein snack, not only for her physical symptoms but also as a crutch and diversion, so I tried to calm her down.

"Carol, have some orange juice or a soft drink and something to eat while you're waiting, and read a book while you're eating." I told her to try and pick out a picture in the book of a comforting scene, and imagine that she was in that scene relaxing.

It worked because she associated herself in a bedroom scene she liked and imagined she was relaxing home in her bedroom and the levels dropped enough for her to stay at least until the hair color was removed and her hair was dry enough to leave. Carol didn't stay to have her hair set and styled that time, but she was able to use her learned techniques the next time and is now able to go to beauty parlors again.

This technique works almost every time if you can just learn to take a deep breath, ride out the flush of anxiety and focus on something in the present, or a comfortable thought that brings you back to a secure feeling once again. The anxiety will subside if you let it!

Chapter Seven

Setting Up An International Pen Pal Club For Agoraphobics And The Buddy System

Since Pat and I had learned there was strength in numbers, and that the secret of recovery was not only in learning the techniques, but mostly in sharing with others how we were coping and growing and learning this recovery.

I put a small ad in the *P.M. News* for a start which read . . ."Wanted: Agoraphobics to write to other Agoraphobics and have your name listed on the current 1982 list . . . . Write ——"

The results were staggering. My mailbox was full every day. I learned that there were other phobia newsletters around the states too, and put the ad in them also. I receive, (even to today) as many as ten letters daily, some six to ten pages long, and then, as now, I write to each and every one individually. Each letter is one asking for help from N.Y. to

Hawaii——each person is reaching out, sharing fears and a very special bond is formed with each. The list was compiled and grew daily to huge proportions (and is still growing). We've become a family unit, knowing, loving one another, and we are sometimes miles and miles apart. But we all wanted names of clinics or self-help support groups in our state, we all wanted to make friends that were phobic possibly in the same city we lived. This is when *The Buddy System* was set up. For example:

There were the young single girls that wrote:

Dear Adele,

". . . . I don't date and that of course is because of my severe agoraphobia. I'm 25 years old, and want to get married someday. What can I do?"

And:

". . . . I'm a 26 year old woman. I have never been married and do not see marriage in the near future. Are there any other agoraphobic women out there who share this problem? I wish I could just meet someone who can share my fears . . . . "

Jill and Kathy both shared the common problem of fear in dating. I was able to direct them both to each other and they have helped one another greatly to say the least of making best friends. Kathy is dating again and has a very understanding boyfriend who is helping her with her problem. Jill lost her boyfriend due to her fear of dating. She now has hope because Kathy is her greatest support!

As the list grew, I was able to "fix up" agoraphobics in the same town by their zip code numbers. Numbers like 11102, 11103, 11004 meant they were close enough to travel to one another's home. This grouping together today has been successful in setting up the support groups in these towns. Many of us can't believe that there are agoraphobics right in our own backyard. I recently found out that there are two agoraphobic women on my block, two on the next block, and five within a radius of six blocks away in my town and more and more are "coming out" and approaching me in the street to ask me about this disease. And to think, five years ago I thought I was going crazy and was "hiding my secret!"

One letter that I received from a woman named Sharon was almost identical to my life story with agoraphobia so much so, I'd like to share it with you, word for word:

"Dear Adele,

I was delighted to receive your letter today and I'm eager as you are, to share anything that might help other agoraphobics.

I am currently in the process of trying to start a local support group for agoraphobics. I was interviewed by a local newspaper last week and my story will be published within two weeks. Another paper printed a letter I wrote to the editor concerning agoraphobia and I've had responses. I've prayed that these articles will reach many sufferers and that the end result will be a group that can minister to one another. I feel I'm a part of a great big family of 'special' people that the Lord is bringing together for the purpose of healing and sharing and loving.

Like you, I'm no longer resentful of all the years living with fear, because the Lord is turning it all into something good. I'm recovering! I feel like a real person again. It's the need to share this with others that's so in my heart.

Psalm 34:4 says, "I have sought the Lord and He answered me and delivered me from all my fears." I have clung to that promise and now am literally seeing it come to pass. It's exciting!

My story, Adele, is probably pretty much the same as most agoraphobics, although I don't have the same strict, rigid childhood background that most phobics have. As best I remember, my parents were reasonably liberal with me. However, I was always a 'high strung' individual even in grade school. My problem really started in high school when I fainted (I could really relate to your story) outside during lunch break, with dozens of kids standing around teasing and laughing when I came to. A police car was dispatched to transport me home, which only attracted even more giggling spectators. I was totally humiliated and dreaded going back to school the next day. Just a few weeks later, I fainted again. This time in the middle of class, and again the classmates made fun. I had a kidney infection at the time of the second fainting spell, so I suppose that could have been responsible.

Anyway, after that second humiliating episode, I was terrified of it happening again, and any slight physical sensation that reminded me of the fainting spells would paralyze me with fear that I was about to pass out. I'd quickly leave the classroom and take refuge at the school nurse's station until I felt in control again. Once in awhile, I would talk the nurse into letting me go home for the day. At this point my fear wasn't severe enough outside the classroom setting to restrict my activities. I was very out going and fairly popular. Things pretty much continued that way until years later when I fainted again. This time I was pregnant with my second child and was shopping in a department store with my mother-in-law. (I also had the flu). When I told my mother-in-law I felt ill, she got me into a nearby employee's lounge where several women were on a break. Just before I lost consciousness, I heard one woman say, 'Oh, God! I hope whatever she has isn't catching!' That was 20 years ago, and her voice and words are just as real to me today. Although I lived with the constant fear of fainting in public, life continued without much restriction for the next five years.

Then in 1968, the panic attacks started. Strangely enough it started at home rather than in a public place. All of a sudden I was beseiged by this horrendous panic and severe depression that never seemed to stop.

It went on all day and all night——sleep was rare and full of terrifying nightmares. All I could do was pace and cry because I was afraid. Afraid of what? I didn't know, but I was sure I would either go crazy or die. My poor husband was totally dismayed. He took me to a medical doctor who told us I had a 'touch of the flu'.

After several more weeks, I became suicidal and was put in a psychiatric ward for five weeks for insulin shock treatments and after release from the hospital, I saw a psychiatrist for a few months. He put me on valium and gradually the fear subsided, but it never went away. That was the real onset of agoraphobia for me.

That was the point in my life when I became terrified of public places, because when I left my house, the fear would escalate and would only subside when I was safely back inside of my house. That was when for the next ten years, I never had a moment of real peace. I functioned better during certain periods than others, but never completely free of fear. I became addicted to valium because it helped me keep my sanity. I was hospitalized again in 1977. During that ten year period, I was put through every kind of psychiatric treatment, including hypnosis, to no avail. My husband spent thousands of dollars and hours of his time dragging me from doctor to doctor, always praying the next one would have the answer. He didn't.

Then around Christmas of 1978, I opened the Sunday edition of our newspaper and read a story. At last I had the answer, or more importantly, a name for my condition. Her symptoms were my symptoms, and it was called agoraphobia. She told about how she'd been helped through a program called TERRAP. Hope at last!

A few weeks later we were transferred here to a Marine Corps base. I was determined to learn everything I could about agoraphobia and I started by reading Claire Week's books. I made some feeble attempts at putting her advice into practice, but didn't gain much ground. I was basically housebound for the next two years, except for occasional courageous ventures out with my husband. (I usually ended up waiting in the car, he did all the shopping.)

In 1981, I wrote TERRAP for information on their programs and subscribed to their terrific newsletter. Suddenly I found myself motivated and determined to become a recovered agoraphobic like the ones I read about in the newsletter. Gradually, I started doing little things; going places with my husband, and once in awhile I'd dare venture out alone close to home.

I started finally telling my friends about my condition and was amazed at their support, love and willingness to help, even though they couldn't fully understand, they cared.

Since then my progress has amazed me, my husband and my friends! I can now drive myself all over the base and even out in town. I do my own shopping and I'm learning to assert myself. I have confidence, I like myself and now I'm reaching out to others with agoraphobia and can't describe the joy! Just today I went to the home of one of the women who contacted me after she read my newspaper article and I spent four wonderful hours telling her that she too can recover. I've also recently found a psychologist who knows about agoraphobia and he is helping me over the rough spots.

Setbacks? Oh, yes! Every day is not a good day. Old behavior patterns rear their ugly heads often, but now, I have the weapons to fight them. And there are still places I can't go and things I can't do alone, but I will someday. For today, I'm thankful for what I can do. I'll be thankful for what I can do tomorrow when tomorrow gets here, however little or how much it may be. I'm still on a low daily dosage of a combination anti-depressant and tranquilizer, but I don't feel guilty about that anymore. I have to remind myself that I'm recovering, not recovered yet. So for right now, I feel okay about the medication and consider it a tool toward ultimate freedom.

I thank God for everything that's taking place in my life. I know He has prepared the way where I walk (or drive) and I thank Him for TERRAP and I thank Him for you. And I thank you for being a willing vessel that He can use to pour out His love to others.

Thank you for letting me share my story. I pray others will be helped.

God Bless you. Dear Adele.

In Christian love, Sharon

This was just one of many beautiful letters in the hundreds and hundreds I received. Sharon is a very special person and you can see, she will recover because she has the desire, fortitude, faith and love to do so. She is a survivor!

As the Buddy System worked, Sharon, Pat and I (as well as many others) were housewives and mothers with similar backgrounds and the love flowed. The bonds could never have been stronger as Pat said this last Thanksgiving, "This year I thank God for helping me overcome Agoraphobia, I thank Him for sending you to me for support and to love, and you truly are my best friend. Without you I never would have come as far as I have!"

As I went on in my research, however, as friends like Michele and another girl named Sharon who was not married, called to my attention, " . . . . I must stress the fact, Adele, that there are many single women and many men that suffer from agoraphobia and it is not merely a 'housewives' condition!"

I had even gotten letters from an eight year old and a seventeen year old who was suffering from agoraphobia. The youngest being a boy, and the latter a young lady!

And, the men who suffered from agoraphobia also felt the pain of it as a letter from Gary, a 24 year old showed:

" . . . . I'm a college graduate with a degree. As early as three years old, I was unable to travel anywhere in a car due to motion sickness. This fear developed into a phobia when just the mention of going somewhere by car, cab, bus, train or any mobile vehicle made me so ill I had to stay home. As I got older, I was only able to go within a few miles from my home. When it was time to get a job, the difficulties increased. Interviews for jobs, meeting with, being with and working with people I had never known before were anticipations of terror.

I did want to progress one step at a time and plunge into a full-time commitment. I decided my first step was temporary employment.

My first job was near home, I then started to graduate and

learn to travel on the trains to the city. Temporary jobs was the answer to my problem at the time because I felt I could accept or reject it. Some jobs might last one day, three weeks, or longer. This allowed me the flexibility to take that first step and has opened up my life for the first time——and has brought me to the point where I can begin looking for something permanent——my career!"

Since Gary had been doing so well and learning how to achieve recovery from agoraphobia, he was just perfect as a "buddy" for two other 24 and 26 year old males I had encountered that lived nearby Gary and suffered from the same fear of traveling far from their home town. Today both Kevin, and Jerry have been helped tremendously by the *Buddy System* and sharing their ups and downs with agoraphobia. The future of a permanent career for all three is looking very bright because they found they were not alone in their fears and there was nothing to be ashamed of even though they were men with a problem to solve!

Perhaps the most moving letters came from Senior Citizens, and Widows who had agoraphobia as a 70 year old phobic, Mildred, wrote: " . . . . I'm a Senior Citizen and very lonely. My husband died, and I have no one. I'm also very sick with high blood pressure and I can't get out to get my medication. I am so severely housebound I can't get out to buy food either. I'm so lonely. What can I do? Please help me, I'm so scared!"

I was so touched by this letter, I found that the local church was delivering meals to Mildred. Dr. Fox, who made housecalls to severe agoraphobics was also the answer for Mildred. And delivery had to be made to her home for medicines until she was well. As far as the loneliness, Buddies and Phobic Aides were also the answer for Mildred's recovery.

Through my newsletter, suggestions for Mildred's recovery came in droves, but one suggestion was perfect. A woman named Frances had suggested that Mildred get a dog. She had been severely phobic and housebound until she went to a local shelter one day and brought home a dog. Naturally, the dog had to be walked a few times a day and this was the answer to an agoraphobic's loneliness too when widowed and alone.

But the one thing I learned through talking with, writing to and meeting agoraphobics, is that we all needed someone and we all needed to be wanted. Being very sensitive, emotional people, depression set in if we felt useless and young or old, male or female, we all strived for the desire to be loved. And we are, if only we can learn to reach out to others, especially others who share our problem in common!

Chapter Eight

Dealing With Setbacks And Resentments

By this time, I had just about completely recovered and had learned how to deal with setbacks and had learned to be independent of Ben and fence for myself in many ways. I had been in an automobile accident coming from an agoraphobic's home. I had been working with her and helping her get out shopping, when a woman hit me broadside after making an illegal U Turn. The first thing I did was check to see if all my ribs were there, the next thing I did was try to open the car door to get out and see what damage there was, but I couldn't open the door it had been damaged so badly. When I got home, I was shook up but was able to get right back into the car to pick Benjie up from school later that day. I didn't let the accident set me backwards and could very easily have given up driving all together. What a shame that would have been after fighting so hard and long to even be able to drive around myself!

I later had an another accident while going down my basement, slipped and broke my ankle. I had been alone at the time, but was able to call an ambulance and get myself to the hospital. I had left a note for Ben and Benjie, that I had broken my ankle and took myself to the hospital in an ambulance to please meet me there when they got home. They thought it had been a joke until they called the hospital! I had grown from a fearful, phobic, once totally housebound and dependent on my husband for everything, to a woman who could finally do things for herself and I was proud.

My broken ankle had come at Christmas time and years ago I would have had the perfect excuse not to go through with Christmas plans and visiting. However, I got a sock over my foot and crutch and all went to my parent's house, and a few other places, (Aunt's, Cousin's) and the next day had Ben's parents, sister, nieces, nephew, and aunt over for dinner, which I cooked while sitting on a stool at the stove and counter top! Nothing and no one was going to stop me anymore! I had learned not to be resentful of ever having had agoraphobia either. In fact, I was glad I had suffered from it, because without ever feeling the pain of agoraphobia, I could never have grown as much and loved others so much, helped them overcome it, or understood the why, how, when, what, and where it originated. I had a complete understanding of agoraphobia now and I wanted to dedicate the rest of my life helping others with it, so why should I resent having ever had it?

For some of us however it took time, as Joan had written on a few occasions of her progress:

" . . . . I debated today if it was the day to answer letters or not, being in a negative, depleted state. I'll give it a go and hopefully not bring you down as I hate to inflict anyone with my down moods. But isn't this the time we need someone who can understand? I've tried everything to live with this fear of mine. Today and many todays like this I feel defeat as I try to find something or someone positive to hold on to. I wish you lived next door to me, you are so positive. I was feeling suicide for a time, but I've no doubt matured some through it all. Burnout seems to be lifting a bit today, but I must go easy in conquering my goals . . . . "

A few months later, Joan was making some progress and wrote:

" . . . Believe this! Have made my fourth visit to the dentist this week! Thank you for the list of other agoraphobics. Just knowing someone is there who understands helps so much! For some of us we must suffer so much before recovering. I sometimes feel like Humpty Dumpty. I keep falling off the wall and getting back up to put myself back together again! . . . . "

And today, Joan is doing fine. She is always ready with the glue she needs to paste back her broken pieces, but she's always fighting and gaining on Agoraphobia!

Resentment and bitterness can sometimes be depleting in setbacks as Judy showed:

" . . . . I had a death in my family and then had to be hospitalized recently. Now, I have come crashing down a month later. I am facing many of the phobias and fears I once had under control. I am afraid again of driving and being away from home. I'm now frightened of taking a planned auto trip to the midwest, even with my family. I do everything I did before but with much more exhaustion and I'm convinced I'll never get through. After all these years of practicing and getting better, I feel I am now taking a giant step backwards. I'm bitter——it's just not fair! Will I ever get back to that level of success I had reached?"

Judy had to learn that her set-back she was experiencing——though painful was only temporary and it would in all probability strengthen her confidence in her ability to keep her phobic situations under control. Her recent tragic experiences were the cause and intensified her old uncertainties, which Claire Weeks said was common and it was to be expected and "accepted in time."

Judy's cure and recovery from her setback was in

recognition of reality and the ability to pursue her goals in the presence of obstacles that were part of reality. Not to recognize this would be a failure to perceive and enjoy the satisfaction and pleasures of growing and accomplishing. Setbacks thus may provide us with opportunities to study negative experiences and construct more realistic beliefs and values and thus achieve more freedom.

Judy is back at her job and doing just fine now. Her setback didn't last very long because she is a fighter!

Sometimes as agoraphobics we fear a setback so much so, every little physical symptom that attacks us and sets us back one step can be devastating and cause us great guilt needlessly as what happened to my best and oldest (not in age) "Buddy", Pat and she wrote:

". . . . I had made a date to meet an old friend for lunch at a restaurant just 20 miles from my home. I was really looking forward to seeing her, but felt sort of 'odd' about two hours before the time to head for the city, but tried to ignore it. I got in the car and started down the expressway. The further I went, the worse I felt. I felt crampy, my back ached, I felt woozy——I knew it was not a panic attack. I have not had one of those terrible things for quite awhile, but I surely would not forget how they felt. No, this was different and the further down the road I went, the worse I felt. Finally I wondered if by some weird chance, this might be a panic attack. The one way to test it is to turn around and head back home. That always makes it go away fast, so even though I was almost at my destination, I turned around and headed back to my home town. But, the more I drove, the worse I felt. I got to the edge of town and pulled into the parking lot of a shopping mall and sat there and waited. I still felt awful, but I was determined to go and meet Sue. I did not want any type of defeat, not after I'd done so well for so long. So, I headed back toward the restaurant a second time and I felt terrible. I finally had to turn around and come home. I felt so bad. I really WANTED to go to see Sue, but I still wondered if maybe somewhere in the back of my mind I was not going through some sort of anxiety attack . . .and yet I knew that was not the case . . . . "

As it was, Pat had been coming down with the flu, as her husband and children did too. So she was not imagining things and wrote in a letter the following week:

" . . . . About my getting sick last week on the road, it was not a panic attack. I had the flu. So, now I am going to go back to just prove I can. I now get 'urges' to get out and get going and do things. That is a new thing for me and I love it! . . ."

Another type of setback can be very upsetting to many of us, and that is the fear of even staying home alone, never mind going outdoors! This sometimes occurrs after a long illness or after being home with small children for a long period of time. But with work, this fear too can be conquered.

Debbie, a young mother of a three year old, had panic attacks while alone at home with her daughter and couldn't wait until her husband came home from work at night because she feared being alone with her child and some terrible doom would overcome them both.

The day unfortunately came, when the baby got very sick and Debbie not only had to get the baby to the hospital, but had to stay in the hospital for three days with her. Debbie had to face a very scary situation alone, without her husband's help because he was out of town. And, by learning she could survive and cope, Debbie finally got the confidence in herself she needed and she is doing fine today!

Another letter from Martha, who's husband was in the service , who shared Debbie's fears:

" . . . . My husband left for a six month tour of duty, so I'm totally on my own. Both children are grown up and gone, it's just me and my two dogs, two cats, and lots of caring friends for support. Of course, my husband is my number one support person, so it's difficult to get used to him not being here, but I've learned enough through the TERRAP program to deal with most anything that comes my way. I can get around pretty good now, do my own shopping, etc. I still have some anxiety about being at home alone, especially at night. Funny, home used to be my 'safe' place until I experienced some very bad panic while home alone. Now it's more of a problem for me than 'out there'. I'm doing quite well though, and know now how to cope with these problems and any setbacks I may encounter!"

And so, setbacks and resentments can be dealt with and put on the back burner, if we only put our minds to it! Right?

Chapter Nine

Traveling Again

One of the hardest things an agoraphobic must overcome in their recovery is traveling to another city by plane, boat, train or a long automobile ride. Once recovering, a phobic may be mobile enough to travel in their town or community, of which my case was. I felt it was time, however, to spread my wings and take on more and difficult tasks. I had become very secure and flexible working in my community and driving in my own town. But I needed to get back into the big city and do some traveling if I was to consider myself really recovered.

An interesting assignment came when a fellow reporter from the newspaper was unable to attend a sports event with big celebrities in another town. When my editor asked me if I'd like to cover it with both pen and camera, I was slightly hesitant, but accepted the challenge.

When the day came, I was a wreck, but determined to take on this assignment. My life had been so boring and secluded as a phobic, the chance of meeting very important celebrities from television was a very exciting aspect.

I had a terrific time, once I warmed up and the nervousness subsided, and met not only sports celebrities, but some prominent politicians as well, who in turn invited me to a political rally to do some publicity articles for my newspaper! This was the beginning of my promotion to Contributing Editor and Photojournalist.

My next big assignment took me to a couple of cities. I had received an invitation to cover a beauty pageant for women over 50, called, *The Golden Girl Beauty Pageant*from the director of the show, Dorothy Dunne. She asked me to be Director of Photography and to write up publicity articles for various magazines and newspapers. Upon accepting this wonderful challenge, I was able to travel to other cities. It was very exciting and I met very interesting people. The first pageant I did had been held in the Prince George Hotel, in N.Y.C. and I had been under some hot camera lights that were being used for Cable T. V. I felt I might be getting an attack at one time, but kept telling myself it was merely the hot lights I was working under with the other cameraman. I was able to get out at a break and get some air, and later returned feeling fine. I had finally learned to give myself the benefit of the doubt and not let my physical feelings overcome me enough to bring me into a real panic attack. I had finally learned the trick to overcome the disease of agoraphobia——but it took nearly five years of hard work!

My husband was proud of me. I could now travel along with him wherever he went. We even went on fishing trips in the Atlantic Ocean on his boat. This was something that scared me into panic at just the thought of being out in a boat with water surrounding me everywhere and no land to run to. But even this became a joy now that I was well again and I really enjoyed going fishing with my husband and son!

Other agoraphobic friends were beginning to do well too and I began to get some encouraging letters from many of my friends I had been making.

Arlene, who had been agoraphobic for many, many years

had been learning to cope. She had found that she was having a problem with sugar intake and after putting herself on a high-protein, low-carbohydrate diet and B vitamins, had felt the enormous change in the way she should cope with her agoraphobia. Diet does affect an agoraphobic! And further research in "chemical imbalances and vitamin deficiecy is now underway!" (See Conclusion notes) Arlene had proved this as well as many other agoraphobics.

She wrote:

"There was a time I couldn't go two miles one way. If I had to stop for a traffic light, I panicked. If men were working on the road and I had to drive through it, I couldn't! I found it so hard to even take my son to boy scout meetings. It was so difficult! But learning to cope is the name of the game. And discipline in my diet! Yesterday, I'm proud to say, however, I took a trip with a few other women from my area to N.Y.C. by bus. We visited all of the sites and I had a ball! I refuse to let agoraphobia run my life... and it feels so good to finally be free of it!"

Shelly, who was having a very difficult time dealing with her fear of traveling by plane and having problems with her husband at the same time because he insisted that she come along with him on business trips. Shelly was desperately afraid of losing her husband, as he constantly threatened divorce. He couldn't understand her fear of flying and she so desperately wanted to overcome the fear, that each trip on the plane, she would deliberately get drunk just to get through it. This, of course, led to more problems, because he got even more upset with her because she couldn't handle her alcohol and was even more of an embarrassment to him when they landed and he had to excuse her from business meetings since she was "hung over" all the time.

Shelly confided, "I knew I had to 'flood myself sober'. By this I mean, I had to go into the feared situation 'cold turkey' if I was ever going to be cured of my fear. So, I took my phobic aide along with me on the next flight. I had a lot of trust in her and knew that my exposure time to the fear would be devastating without her."

But this method worked for Shelly. Although flooding a phobic with exposure to the very thing she fears, can prove to be extremely hard work, in this case it was just what she needed to overcome the fear. Every time Shelly avoided the one thing she feared by dulling herself from any physical sensations with alcohol, she made her phobia worse than it was before, and the next time back on the plane, facing the fear again, became even more difficult. So, Shelly learned with her phobic aide, that through relaxation, diversion and facing her fear, she could overcome it without even drinking an ounce of alcohol.

I get post cards now and then from Shelly. Last one was from Hawaii. " . . . . I'm having a wonderful time, the trip was fine!"

Many men phobics, turn down good jobs or chances for advancement in their companies because of the fear to travel away from their secure home town office. This is usually the most common form of agoraphobia in men.

But through practice, encouragement from a buddy or phobic aide, this fear can be dealt with effectively.

TERRAP which I've mentioned quite often in these latter pages, is a program (address at back of book) that eventually takes agoraphobics on "vacations" with other agoraphobics and aides. This is a very special program designed to help the recovering phobic become more flexible and take on a broader environment and help them to cope with any anxiety in a controlled situation.

Agoraphobics no longer have to fear traveling today because of these wonderful methods available to them no matter if they are male or female.

And there are many ways of setting up these organizations right in your own home town as I will explain in this following chapter . . . . . .

Chapter Ten

Setting Up A Support Group In Your Town

Fact number one being that an agoraphobic who is severely ill with the disease cannot get anywhere too far from home to receive help is what encouraged me to ask Dr. Stephan Fox, PH. D. to help me set up some sort of Support Group Sessions, a Newsletter, and housecalls to severe agoraphobics housebound in our area.

I had met Dr. Fox by putting an ad in the newspaper I worked for. And through meeting him, a group was set up, a newsletter and housecalls were arranged as well as my already growing International Pen-Pal Club and Hotline.

I began to get letters from my friends throughout the U.S. who wished they too lived nearby so they could benefit from this sort of support system. I wrote to each one and new groups began to flourish from my idea in different states. Pat, who had been growing rapidly in recovery was ready to start a group in her town. She called her local newspaper and asked to be interviewed by their staff reporter. A wonderful article came out, and two days later, she was flooded with phone calls and set up H.O.P.E. (Help Overcome Phobic Experiences) and a H.O.P.E. Hotline where phobics could call when they needed reassurance or help. She was able to get the pastor of her church to lend out the hall to hold the meetings and today H.O.P.E. is doing wonderful things. Not too long ago both Pat and I met through a phobic newsletter and were both severely agoraphobic and handicapped. Today we are running groups as moderators!

As Pat quoted in her newspaper article, "...the key to my current freedom from the terror of agoraphobia was identifying the problem and striking up a meaningful friendship with a New York victim by phone and mail, named Adele. She is my best friend next to my husband, and I've never even met her yet! We have played one-upmanship with each other for the past few years and are both recovered. I would describe a monumental drive to the book store and she would write back that she had driven just one mile further and had gotten out and looked in the store window, which made me strive to go into the store in my town and purchase a book .... "

It was the support that was the key!

Sharon, who had once shared her heartbreaking letter we've read in a latter chapter was now recovered too and wrote:

" .... I've started a local self-help group here with other agoraphobics. We don't have a professional therapist or priest heading it up like you and Pat do, but my therapist has promised to come and speak to the group on several "guest appearances" and we are working on having other professionals too. We keep meetings at each other's houses, and keep in daily touch by phone and go out together as a group on outings holding one another together like glue. We call our group, P.A.L.S. (Partners in Agoraphobic Life

Support) It's growing daily, just by a local write up in our newspaper and posters in the supermarket! . . . . "

The best way to start a group in your town is to use the local media, church, newspaper, local store posters, etc. A good idea is to get a post office box too for mail so that you don't run into problems with annoyance calls at your doorstep. Pat had made the mistake of giving her home address in the newspaper article and found women knocking at her door at un-opportune times.

I suggest you have a co-moderator who is recovered, and it is very helpful to have a licensed psychologist available to help if possible.

The meetings should not last longer than an hour and some refreshments such as juice or coffee and cake could help to insure a comfortable atmosphere. Assure incoming members that they can bring husbands, boyfriends, etc. any support person they may feel can help if they need to. You will later see the group will want to share in the responsibility of being a co-leader. Encourage this and give each a turn to help run the meeting is vital to their recovery to feel needed and assertive!

Very important no-no's to remember when running a group is that there should be no put-downs, gossip or accusatory remarks. Each should be assured of her privacy in certain matters and should not feel guilty if they are not ready to share a personal problem. Most of all there should be no symptom swapping. Others will pick up on them and the whole group will pick up on them. One should remind another if this happens and politely change the subject.

There should be an interesting topic of discussion each week, and some time left to share success stories for encouragement each week and all should set up goals for the next week. If someone is too shy to speak up during the meeting, don't push. Allow them to "pass" until they feel more comfortable talking before the group.

A group newsletter can be set up when possible and there should be typewritten materials to give out. For this, a basket should be passed around for donations toward the coffee, cake, etc, and printing and duplicating costs.

Shy or gregarious, open or closed, each member will be helped by his exposure to the group's collective support. The group will steadily make steps toward freedom. An agoraphobic can only grow by attending support groups and talking with other agoraphobics, there is no denying this!

As a group you will see other's growth, share each other's defeats and pick one another back up and set their fellow buddy back on the road to success.

With the group's support and through applaud, each agoraphobic will make confident strides to complete independence and recovery.

In the following pages, I have given you examples of how I typed out and photostated my letters and announcements here in my town for examples for you to follow:

Good luck with your group!

You no longer have to live with crippling diseases caused by fears and phobias!

We are forming a support group for people with phobias now. This will be led by two experienced people on this topic, Dr. Stephan Fox, Licenses Psychotherapist, and Adele Paolino, co-leader, and former recovered agoraphobic.

For any housebound agoraphobics, housecalls will be arranged and phobic aids are available to help you overcome the feared situtation. The techniques used will be: relaxation, behaviorial modification, desensitization, support, encouragement, clarification, ventilation, and other appropriate means.

If you're interested, please contact Dr. Stephan Fox.

Stephan Fox, PH.D., C.S.W.
993 Park Avenue
New York, N.Y. 10028

WE HAVE GREAT NEWS! Dr. Fox and I have decided to print a new monthly newsletter for phobics, called, "Personally Yours News." It is a new dimension in newsletters for agoraphobics, because YOU write it. Our concept is different in that you can reach many other agoraphobics by your letters. By sharing our feelings and experiences with others who understand, we can begin to grow and recover! We will print your articles, and letters in order to help and support each other on an international basis.

Each month, Dr. Fox will answer any questions you may have, and there will be different tips on how you can learn to cope with phobias and completely learn how to overcome these fears.

Unlike other newsletters that cost as much as $75.00 a month for this same service, ours will cost only $10.00 a year.

So, fill in the attached form and mail your letters, articles, puzzles, cartoons as well as any classified ads you would like to place. All ads are free of charge!

"PERSONALLY YOURS NEWS" IS YOUR NEWSLETTER, SO PLEASE SUPPORT IT!

....

Yes. I want to receive PERSONALLY YOURS NEWS. Here is my check for 1 year subscription for $10.00 made payable to Adele Paolino, Editor

NAME..

ADDRESS...

....

TELEPHONE ....
(area code)

Hi,
I'm announcing the beginning of my new self-help group for phobias to be held at my house on Friday evenings at 7 p.m. to 9 p.m. weekly.

I plan on making these meetings a relaxed, party-type gathering where we can share out problems, support one another, and perhaps even laugh at our shortcomings.

There will be no charge other than the kitty for donations for coffee and cake, and wine and cheese, plus the printed material I will be handing out at each meeting. This will consist of all the latest techniques and news about combating phobias.

So please call me if you'd like to join.

Love,

Adele

Conclusion

Agoraphobia——the strange malady which has been described as a terror for millions, plaguing both men and women, no longer has to cripple minds.

Guilt, once caused these victims of this disease, to hide behind closed doors, in shame. Some of us lived in terror of going insane, for some of us we thought we were already insane. This no longer has be be the case. Today there are numerous places where one can get help in their own town. And, if the case may be, that there is no group, or clinic in your area to help agoraphobics, many strides are being made to set these groups and clinics up. Help is out there, and no one has to suffer with agoraphobia anymore.

I'd like to personally thank every one who wrote me with their case histories in my research, sharing their deepest fears and secrets to come out into the open sharing these insecurities with others in order to help. I'd especially like to thank all my dearest friends, whom I've met throught my recovery; Pat, Joan, Jill, Michele, Sharon, Kathy, Ernestine, Valerie, Arlene, Mary, Frances, Debbie and many, many more who have become life-long "buddies" sharing step-by-step recovery methods, rewarding each other with support, and the special love, understanding, and caring only another agoraphobic could understand.

Special thanks to Dr. Stephan Fox, PH. D. C.S.W., who came forth in the N.Y.C. area and agreed to make 'housecalls' to housebound agoraphobics and saw the need to visit severe cases in order to get them back out and on their feet to recovery.

Special thanks to my husband and family for sticking by me when I was down, and having faith in my project.

IT WAS ONLY WITH SUCH SUPPORT AND LOVE THAT I RECOVERED COMPLETELY FROM THE CLUTCHES OF AGORAPHOBIA1

Following is a list of places to get help if there is nowhere in your immediate area . . . . . .

WHERE TO GET HELP FOR AGORAPHOBIA

The Phobia Clinic, White Plains Hospital Medical Center
P.M. News
Davis Avenue
White Plains, N.Y. 10601

TERRAP
T.S.C. Corp.
1010 Doyle St.
Menlo Park, CA 94025

Lifeline
Phobia Resource Center
1430 Second Avenue
Suite 109
New York, N.Y. 10021

Dr. Stephan Fox, Ph.D, C.S.W.
993 Park Avenue
New York, N.Y. 10028

Dr. Manuel Zane (Contextual Therapy)
c/o White Plains Phobia Clinic
Davis Avenue
White Plains, N.Y. 10601

Personally Yours News & International Phobic Pen Pal Listing
c/o Adele Paolino, Editor
P.O. Box 92
Ft. Tilden, N.Y. 11695

H.O.P.E.
680 W. Summit
Alliance, Ohio 44601

Living Growth Program
A Resort For Agoraphobics
2000 Idylwild
Prescott, Arizona 86301

Author's Note

I hope this book has been of help to you, and I thank you for purchasing it and reading it. In the future I have hopes to publish a sequel and need your comments. How would you feel about a book containing all case histories of other agoraphobics and how they are coping, recovering, etc? Also, I need more MALE case histories. I'd also like to include recent research on chemical imbalance, vitamin therapy and nutrition and how it affects agoraphobia. How do you feel about this topic? Please write to me at the following address with your comments and case histories. If you'd like to share your story with others, jot it down and send it to me, especially if you have found a special way to recovery. All names and personal addresses, etc, will be kept strictly confidential in the book...

Also, if you'd like to subscribe to the International Pen Pal Club for Agoraphobics send $2.50 and a #10 Self Addressed-Stamped Envelope (SASE) to me at the following address. And if you'd like to subscribe to the newsletter, *Personally Yours News* fill out the following form and mail it with a $10.00 check to:

PYN
ADELE PAOLINO, EDITOR
P.O. BOX 92
FT. TILDEN, N.Y. 11695

.... Yes, I'd like to subscribe to *Personally Yours News*. Here is my $10.00 for 12 monthly newsletters.

Name: ______________________________

Address: ______________________________

Telephone: ______________________________

....

Copies are $5.95 plus $1.25 for postage and handling.

Please send me copies of "Agoraphobia. How I Overcame This Crippling Disease." Payable to Adele Paolino, P.O. Box 92. Ft. Tilden, N.Y. 11695

NAME ....

ADDRESS: ....

....

*All copies are guaranteed.
An Apollo Book
263 W. 5th St.
Winona, MN 55987